Loose Cow Party

by

Baxter Black

*To The "John Wayne" of
my Dreams... David !!
Love, Charli
Christmas, 1998
Edmonds, Washington
at
Christmas Cow Party time!*

illustrated by Don Gill, Bob Black and Charlie Marsh

COYOTE COWBOY COMPANY

BENSON, ARIZONA 1998

All poems written by Baxter Black

Copyright © 1998 by Baxter Black

Published by Coyote Cowboy Company
P.O. Box 2190
Benson, Arizona 85602

LIBRARY OF CONGRESS CATALOGING IN PUBLICATION DATA

Main entry under:
Cowboy Poetry

Bibliography: p
1. Coyote Cowboy Poetry
2. Cowboy-Poetry
3. Poetry-Cowboy
4. Humor-Cowboy
5. Agriculture-Poetic Comment

I. Black, Baxter, 1945-

Library of Congress #98-072674
ISBN 0-939343-29-0

OTHER BOOKS BY BAXTER

* THE COWBOY AND HIS DOG © 1980
* A RIDER, A ROPER AND A HECK'UVA WINDMILL MAN © 1982
ON THE EDGE OF COMMON SENSE, THE BEST SO FAR © 1983
* DOC, WHILE YER HERE © 1984
BUCKAROO HISTORY © 1985
COYOTE COWBOY POETRY © 1986
✔ CROUTONS ON A COW PIE © 1988
✔ THE BUCKSKIN MARE © 1989
✔ COWBOY STANDARD TIME © 1990
CROUTONS ON A COW PIE, VOL 2 © 1992
HEY, COWBOY, WANNA GET LUCKY? *(Crown Publishing, Inc.)* © 1994
DUNNY AND THE DUCK © 1994
COW ATTACK © 1996
CACTUS TRACKS AND COWBOY PHILOSOPHY *(Crown Publishing, Inc.)* © 1997

* included complete in Coyote Cowboy Poetry 1986
✔ included compete in Croutons On A Cow Pie, Vol 2 1992

TABLE OF CONTENTS

ALL RANCH RODEO 60

BOTH SIDES 30

FAIRBOARD 12

FEEDLOT HEROES 38

HELPLESS 32

HORSE SHOW CONVERSATION 20

HOW DO YOU KNOW IT'S CHRISTMAS 50

IF HEREFORDS WERE BLACK 14

ILLINOIS COWBOY 10

JOHNNY WAS A MULE MAN 48

LOOSE COW PARTY 4

LOOSE IN THE SALE BARN 18

MR. DEWEY'S HOOK AND CHAIN 44

NIGHT MAN IN THE HEIFER LOT 34

OUTFITTER'S JERKY 22

POWER PROFESSIONAL PROCESSING TEAM 24

PROLAPSE FROM THE BLACK LAGOON 8

PROUD CUT HOLSTEIN STEER 28

RC & BUD 56

RHINO LOVE 42

SALESMAN'S DILEMMA 58

SAMARITAN ANGEL 46

SANTY'S EMISSION STICKER 52

SPRINGTIME IN THE ROCKIES 6

TED'S BIG STEER 36

THERAPEUTIC GOAT 54

VEGETABLE DEFAMATION TRIAL 40

VISITING DOGS 26

WAITING FOR DADDY 16

WATER 33

LOOSE COW PARTY

"It's for you," his darlin' told him as he lay back in the chair
For a well deserved siesta. Ugh, it wasn't really fair.
It was Chuck, his nearest neighbor - did he have to call right now?
Millard took the phone and listened, "Are you sure that it's my cow?"

As if he'd changed his brand last week or something equally absurd
Like the F.B.I. was posing as a member of his herd
Or an alien invasion took possession of his place
And planned to infiltrate the earth as cows from outer space.

But no easy explanation seemed to ease his heavy load.
Chuck said, "Better come and get her, she's a'grazin' on the road."
Saddled up, he hit the highway and broke into a jog
With his wife not far behind him in the pickup with the dog.

He could spot the cow's location from within a half a mile.
Cars were backed up to the corner, everybody wore a smile.
Helpful tourists waved and hollered, horsemen galloped to and fro
Swingin' ropes like polo players, someone takin' video.

Millard rode into the melee as the cow turned up the lane.
She trompled through the clothesline draggin' laundry like a train
Through the hogwire to the garden, through the hotwire to the corn,
'Cross the rows with cornstalks flyin', laundry hangin' off her horn.

There were fifteen mounted riders rattlin' through the stubble field,
Millard got a rope around her but he knew his fate was sealed
When he felt the horn knot grabbin' and the saddle slip an inch . . .
He remembered he'd forgotten to retighten up his cinch.

He was still there in the saddle but it now sat on the neck.
We should pause and take reflection while we visualize the wreck. *(pause)*
Millard peeled off the equine like a dirty undershirt
He was still tall in the saddle when his boot heels hit the dirt.

You could think of water skiing. You could think of Roto-Till
But when fifteen mounted riders mash you flat, it's all downhill.
Millard watched from his position in the furrow that he'd plowed
While the cow crashed through the hotwire, disappearin' in the crowd.

There the band of merry revelers in gesture grandiose
Lashed up the draggin' rope somehow, around a solid post.
The crowd began to dissipate. It was over, they could sense
Leavin' Millard to apologize to Chuck about his fence.

4

Chuck was gracious. Millard thanked him for his helpfulness and such
    But it seemed like Chuck enjoyed it . . . just a little bit too much.
But he really couldn't blame him. When a loose cow wreck occurs
    It's a miserable fiasco, less of course, it isn't yers!

SPRINGTIME IN THE ROCKIES

When it's springtime in the Rockies
and my lips are turning blue
I'll be slogging through the blizzard
like a brain dead caribou....

Ah, springtime.
That first hint of life beginning anew, the annual transformation,
the earth taking off its long johns, shedding its skin,
clearing its throat in long tubercular coughs that turn rain into birdshot,
sleet into ice, ice into snowflakes shaped like goatheads or bob wire,
not falling but slicing by you like shrapnel, sandblasting your face,
freezing your rein hand into a claw and turning forty-five degrees and balmy
into assault with intent to stupefy.

Ah, springtime.
Brave wild flowers bursting from winter's blanket, the trill of the mountain bluebird,
the exultation of a rushing brook, the whine of a spinning tire,
the splock of pliers dropped from your hand, the rattle of mudtags on a feedlot steer
that makes him sound when he walks like a limping Moroccan bride.
That half brave, half scared elation of aiming your truck toward the muddy dirt road ruts
like a boat captain docking with the current, like Fast Eddy runnin' one down the rail.

Ah, springtime.
The anticipation of a new bride or a butterfly waking in his cocoon.
Like Christmas Eve with all the presents of summer waiting to be opened.
The weatherman declaring winter's over, angels celebrating the vernal equinox
by hosing out Gabriel's hog confinement shed,
Drip drying their laundry between the mountain tops and revving up the windchill machine
for one last recalibration.

Ah, springtime,
Best viewed through a picture window settin' by the fire.

Once again you'll hear me promise
You'll be hearing from me soon.
When it's springtime in the Rockies
I'll be calling from Cancun...

PROLAPSE FROM THE BLACK LAGOON

It came from outta nowhere, like a prolapse in the night.
      Which, in fact is what it was my friends, the cow vet's scourge and plight.
   That pudgy pink projectile from those monster movie scenes
      Like some whopping giant burrito filled with attitude and beans.

I was soon laid down behind it on a hillside in the muck
      While the cowboy shined his high beams from his perch there in the truck.
   His rope stretched from the bumper to her front legs tied in haste.
      As I wallowed in the darkness like a frog, stripped to the waist.

It was bigger than a tree trunk. It was slick as old chow mein.
      It was heavy as a carpet someone left out in the rain.
   I tried to gain some purchase as I pressed my fist in tight,
      It was like a thrashing porpoise and was putting up a fight.

I got it in a hammerlock. It was like a rabid dog.
      I wrapped my legs around it like a monkey on a log.
   I pushed until my shoulder disappeared inside the mass
      As I scrabbled for a foothold in the mud and frozen grass.

But alas, with one huge effort she expelled me from her grip.
I shot out like a cannon, rolled and did a double flip
But I grabbed her tail in passing and with strength born out of war,
I dove at the appendage like some punch drunk matador.

I lifted her hind quarters, and I swung her side to side,
Then, like smart men do...I used my head, to push it back inside!
It was dark there for a second, it was hard to catch my breath
But there she lay, my patient I had saved from certain death.

The cowboy rolled his window down, said, "Doc, are you alright?"
He gunned the engine several times. The headlights got real bright.
"I've seen a prolapse done before but never quite like that!"
"Oh, they taught us that in vet school...But I think it ate my hat."

ILLINOIS COWBOY

"Where were you born?" The reporter asked one of my Colorado cowboy friends.

"Iowa," he answered.

"Iowa!" she said. "Why did you move?"

"Because it's hard to be a cowboy in Iowa."

Well, it might be harder to be a cowboy in the Midwest but they've got a bunch of good ones anyway. No matter how much dependence modern cowmen place on man-made mechanical devices, there are times when nothin' beats a good roper a'horseback.

Illinois is an anthill of bovine activity. They have an abundance of cow calf operations and the state has ranked in the top ten in numbers of cattle on feed. So a "loose cow" is not an unusual occurrence. That's when a good cowboy comes in handy.

Dr. Matt has his veterinary clinic in one of the many small towns that dot the northwestern Illinois countryside. One afternoon he was processing a truckload of feeder steers in the back of his clinic.

Despite good help and good facilities, accidents can happen. A gate was left open and shornuf, one of the steers escaped. And, according to Rule #1 in the _Guidebook of Loose Cattle_, the steer headed straight for the center of town.

Matt leaped to his Toyota Batmobile and took up the chase as the girls in the office cheered him on and wished, not for the first time, they'd had a video camera.

The steer had the advantage. He was able to cut through lawns, across lots filled with farm implements, behind gas pumps and down sidewalks. He jaywalked with impunity.

He galloped into the bank drive-thru, raised his tail to the pie-eyed teller and proceeded to circle the bank building. Matt careened into the drive-thru hot on the trail. By using the parking lot and surrounding sidewalks, he was able to keep the steer circling the bank through the manicured lawn and decorative shrubbery.

Matt's radio crackled, "Chet's just pulled into the clinic, could you use some help?"

The steer broke for the high school. "Send him on," Matt yelled, "we're headed for the football field!"

The steer had slowed to a trot by the time Chet wheeled his pickup and trailer into the school parking lot. He unloaded his horse, grabbed his rope and mounted.

Matt said it was beautiful to watch. When Chet rode through the goal posts the steer was on the twenty yard line and pickin' up speed.

Chet's horse was kickin' up big divots and Chet was leaning forward like an outside linebacker. He sailed his loop and nailed the steer on the fifty yard line. An amazing catch.

The grandstands were empty. Nobody saw it but Matt, and he told me, with a faraway look in his eye, that to this day he can still hear the roar of the crowd.

THE FAIRBOARD

It was every fairboard's nightmare when the lightning hit the stage.
    'Course, it might have been expected; it was just another page
In a trail of disasters that befell our county fair
    That began when Dr. Knockwurst told us we should be aware

That a stomatitis outbreak might shut down the rodeo
    Not to mention all the entries in the Junior Livestock Show.
Then the day before we opened they began to excavate
    Down the center of the highway that runs up to the main gate.

Of course, they hit a waterline. We were Lake Louise by dawn.
    But no water in the spigots in the barns or in the john.
So we planned on shuttle parking using pontoons and canoes
    But we finally wound up asking folks to just take off their shoes.

And the carnival got testy 'cause we couldn't build a bridge
    Plus the vendors all were grumblin' due to decreased patronage
But the tractor pull went okay 'cept they pulled a light pole down
    Which played havoc with the dog trials when two handlers almost drowned.

On the morning of the last night the promoter called to say
    That the singer had a sore throat and could not perform, no way.
But by noon it didn't matter 'cause the clouds came rollin' in
    And the crowd all left in lifeboats so by five we pulled the pin.

We retreated to the office down beneath the grandstand seats
    Where the fairboard did its business and hashed out the balance sheets.
'Cause tonight we were survivors. Like a pile of used retreads
    Only glad that it was over, all we did was shake our heads

And ask ourselves why anyone would take this thankless chore
    When a kid, in tow with mother, stuck his head in through the door.
He had lost his yellow ribbon, she explained, both drippin' pools,
    And wondered if by some small chance, if it weren't against rules...

Could we? "Course we could!" I shouted. "We're the fairboard! That's our thing!"
    So we picked him out a dry one. It was like we crowned him king.
And he tried to say his thank you's but his tears got in the way.
    Time stood still as he departed. No one had too much to say

'Til the lightning hit the stage lights, then I heard me volunteer,
    "I reckon we should get them fixed 'fore we do much else next year."

IF HEREFORDS WERE BLACK

If Herefords were black and Angus were red
    would breeders of Herefords breed Angus instead?
I mean, would the people who bred Herefords first
    be now breeding Angus if things were reversed.

    Or would they be loyal to red, white and true
        To color of cowlick be always true blue?
    If such were the case would they dis all the blacks,
        Tell jokes about prolapse, compare them to Yaks

More suited for saddle or wearin' a yoke
    Than stubbornly breeding until they go broke.
And those of the Aberdeen Angus cartel,
    would they tout maternal endowments, as well,

    Promoting their native resistence to thorns,
        while cursing as mutants those not sprouting horns.
    Just draggin' their sheath through the cheatgrass and burrs
        like leaky ol' bass boats nobody insures.

Debate would rage on like it does anyway
    if South had worn blue or the North had worn gray,
Or if Henry Ford had been Hank Chevrolet
    You'd still be a Ford man... or would you, today?

    So if Herefords were black and Angus were red
        would breeders of Herefords breed Angus instead?
    The question begs deep philosophical thought
        but don't get disgruntled or get overwrought

The breeders of purebreds run true to the grain
    And efforts to change them would just be in vain
And not 'cause they think other cattle are bad
    "I'm stickin' with this one, 'cause that's what Dad had."

WAITING FOR DADDY

"Mama, when's Daddy comin' home? Is it time to worry yet?"
"By supper, darlin'. Eat your Cheerios."
> *He rode out this morning early. Like he does six days a week*
> *I always make him tell me where he goes*
> *'Specially when I know he's headed over on the canyon side*
> *At least I know I'll have a place to start*
> *So in case he doesn't come back I can hunt for him myself*
> *Or go for help if I get faint of heart*

"Run and git your schoolbooks, kiddos! And be sure to wash yer hands."
"Aw Mama, do we have to school today?"
> *If it wasn't for home schooling I might lose what mind I've got*
> *It helps to pass the daylight time away*
> *And I know I shouldn't worry but I worry anyway*
> *Who wouldn't, if they were in my shoes*
> *I've been up those rocky canyons and I've seen those snaky trails*
> *I know how quick a horse can blow a fuse*

"Mama, Cody said a swear word." "I did not!" "Did too!" "Did not!
I only said Ring went to the commode."
> *Oh, thank God I've got these children just to keep me occupied*
> *But still I'm always lookin' down the road*
> *All afternoon I've watched the sky. It's like I'm playin' poker*
> *You don't know how I fear an angry cloud*
> *And the wind gives me the shivers. Never lets me drop my guard.*
> *Nothin' like it whispers quite so loud*

"Mama, when's Daddy comin' home? Shouldn't he be home by now?
We wanna ride before it gets too dark."
> *And the hardest time for me I guess is now till six o'clock*
> *I'm nervous till I hear the home dogs bark*
> *But the kids are my salvation. 'Course, they wanna be like Dad*
> *He saddles up their horse and lets'em go*
> *And I stand here by the window thinkin' 'here we go again'*
> *But they're cowboyin', the only life they know*

"Mama, look! Oh, here comes Daddy. That's him trottin' up the road.
He's wavin', now he's comin' through the gate."
> *"See, I told you kids be patient, not to get your dander up . . ."*
> *And learn to wait, and wait and wait and wait.*

LOOSE IN THE SALE BARN

They weren't in the habit of raisin' wild cattle in that part of Michigan, so the fences aren't that high. But when the heifer cruised into the sale ring like a shark in to the kiddie pool, everybody knew they might not be high enough.

As the bidding began she never slowed, but circled the ring scatterin' cowboys, plastic whips, rubber boots and cups of coffee. One of the cowboys ducked behind the wooden screen just as the heifer planted one big paw on its top and vaulted over the rails into the crowd.

The Marion sale barn was packed that day. Jim was one of the buyers who worked for the facility. He watched from the walkway at the top, back behind the bleacher seats as the heifer climbed the stairs six at a time headin' his way.

The crowd was plenty excited. Folks were yellin' and clearin' a path. The bidding had stopped at seventy-five cents.

The heifer weighed less than 500 lbs and was a Limousin mountain goat cross. When she leveled out on the walkway at the summit of the sale barn, all those gathered in the back were lookin for a hole! She raced back and forth between the solid walls of concrete on one side and the solid wall of farmers on the other, occasionally smearing a dab of green about waist high.

Jim was mashed in the crowd watching when suddenly he recalled... "Wait a minute? I work for the company!"

"Let's get her, Larry, before somebody gets hurt!"
"How?" asked Larry, who was sort of enjoying the diversion.

"I don't know!" hollered Jim, who then dove on the heifer as she made her next pass. They went down and skidded in a pile. Larry, who was almost as big as the heifer, fell on Jim. It knocked the breath outta all three of them.

A regular, who'd enjoyed the show, whipped off his dress belt and made a collar around the calf's neck. Jim and Larry wallered her around awhile by the collar and tail 'til someone brought'em a good chunk of rope. As they started out the door with the heifer, the original owner shouted, "Hold on! She's not sold yet!"

Jim hollored back through the door, "Seventy-six!"
The gavel came down.

Two days later they ran the heifer through the sale ring again still wearin' the rope. She brought sixty cents.

Jim was in the ring and asked the buyer, "Can I have my rope back?"
"Sorry, son," The buyer said, "that's the only reason I bought the heifer!"

18

THE HORSE SHOW CONVERSATION

"A fine lookin' horse you've got there *(if yer into modern art)*
  I had a horse like that one time *(but he wasn't very smart)*

  I'd guess that he's part thoroughbred *(and part Catahoula hound)*
    You get him in a claiming race? *(or at the lost and found)*

Oh, really, you've got the papers *(I'd use'em to train the dog)*
  And he's outta He's California! *(No wonder he smells like smog)*

  He seems a little bit feisty *(to have one foot in the grave)*
    Yup, I've used Ace myself sometimes *(when there's somethin' left to save)*

What kinda bit have you got there? *(it looks like a calving tool)*
  Oh, you invented it yourself *(Do them Vise Grips make him drool?)*

  Yeah, I'll bet it sure does stop him *(like runnin' into a train)*
    You must of built that tie-down, too *(Never seen one made outta chain)*

And where did you get those leggin's? *(from a circus refugee)*
  Well, most people like'm longer *(At least down to the knee)*

  Good luck. I reckon yer up soon *(I'd hate to be in that wreck)*
    You've already finished your class? *(And haven't broken yer neck)*

Two firsts and honorable mention! *(Whoa up! I'm way off the trail!)*
  A fine lookin' horse you've got there *(maybe that sucker's for sale...)*

THE OUTFITTER'S JERKY

In hunting camp an outfitter leaned down and stirred the fire.
    His client belched contentedly and said, "Might I inquire,
That jerky you been chewin' on... could I just try a bit?
    I fancy I'm a connoisseur with tongue and palate fit
        To ferret out the kind of beast, perhaps the cut of meat
            From whence you sliced the bloody strap and held it to the heat."
    The packer passed a little piece to test the boastful claim,
        The hunter sniffed the charred remains, bit in and then proclaimed,

"I taste a hint of kidney fat. The tang of creosote.
    A wistful note of pine tree sap lays pungent in my throat.
What's this? A waft of ungulate, the glue of hoof and horn,
    An Eohippus redolence, the musk of unicorn.
        Peculiar, though I must admit, I can't tell heads nor tails.
            I'm left with just the essence of burnt hair and roofing nails.
        I pride myself on this small skill but if you could be swayed,
            Pray, tell me from what animal is this here jerky made?"

The packer picked his grimy teeth, his filthy knife, the tool.
    "It all began," he spit and said, "with one ol' stubborn mule
Named Demon, and the name sure fit. Worst mule I've ever seen.
    Last hunt when we were comin' out he really got down mean.
        It took us nearly half a day to git the sucker packed.
            He'd buck the panyards off each time and roll clear on his back.
        He kicked and struck and strained the knots, he bit and brayed and gassed,
            We finally had to tie him down to get the elk made fast.

At last he stood and glared at us, resigned but not unbowed.
    We started down the mountain side as best the load allowed.
We had to cross a narrow trail above a closed down mine.
    The Demon went to pullin' back, I'd hitched him last in line.
        He balked, then had a mental lapse... forgot that he was tied!
            And then just like a fumbled punt he cartwheeled down the side.
        I quit my horse and bared my knife, and dove between the mules.
            I slashed the halter shank between the mule train and the fools.

Down we went, an avalanche of elk and mule and man,
    The antlers racked the Coleman stove, I kissed the frying pan.
The propane tank was hissin', the elk meat held on tight,
    I hit the shale below the mine, the mule dropped outta sight.
        Above my head a blinding flash exploded in my eyes.
            And when the dust had settled, the mule had vaporized.
        I peeked down in the mine shaft through the timbers and the smoke
            And saw ol' Demon at long last had shed his final yoke.

He never knew what hit him, so at least it wasn't cruel."
   "Gosh," the hunter shook his head, "I'm sorry 'bout yer mule.
But back to this here jerky, do you share your recipes?"
   "Well, wuddn't nuthin' to it. I just picked it off the trees."

THE POWER PROFESSIONAL PROCESSING TEAM

It struck in late October like a plague of mustard gas.
It started with a trickle but then soon began to mass
In pens and cattle alleys on the new receiving side.
The fall run was beginning and there was no place to hide.
The boss said "Git'em processed, just as fast as they come in!
A crew'll bring'em to ya and then take'em back again."
So, K.T. got three cowboys and headed toward the shed,
"You shovel out the squeeze chute, Clyde. Juan, come with me," she said.

They filled a gooseneck trailer with the stuff she thought they'd need.
"We'll inventory later, right now, all that counts is speed!"
By eight the chute was bangin' through the second semi load.
The cattle to be processed stretched a mile down the road.
Syringes on the fast draw firin' doses of vaccine,
Hydraulic handles flippin' like a bad pinball machine,
Blue smoke and buzzin' bee stings from the hotshots and the brands,
An ear tag like a snake bite, bawlin' calves and flashin' hands,

An implant undercover, some pour on down the back,
Dewormer for the pore ones, dehorning with a crack.
Release the head, a clatter. Release the squeeze, a pause.
He bolts, but then the next one is captured in the jaws.
On and on they processed 'til their hands were just a blur,
The cattle like a carousel, the headgate just a whir.
Above the shed an aura that so brightened up the skies
The cowboys bringin' new ones had to cover up their eyes.

A vacuum was created like a swirlin' whirlwind.
As soon as one was turned out, it sucked the next one in.
The final bunch was brought up but when the last one fled
They couldn't quit, their auto pilot stuck full speed a-head!
They might have gone forever 'cept the power went haywire.
The crew walked out like robots whose brains had caught on fire.
They stood around unknowing, ears still ringin' from the fray,
So numb they could remember nothing that transpired that day.

But driftin' in next morning came the news of all they'd done,
Two thousand head they'd processed, caught and treated every one,
Plus, a hundred saddle horses, the neighbor's feeder pigs,
A pair of tawdry mannequins with English lawyer wigs,
A marching band from Goodland, sixteen greyhounds from the track,
The local Veterans Color Guard, a llama and a yak,
Assorted order buyers and a great big plastic steer,
Not to mention one truck driver with a lot tag in his ear.

Reports just kept on comin' from the countryside around.
The feedlot was a'buzzin' with each new add-on they found,
But Boss, he saw things different, "K.T., what about the cost?
Them extra ones you processed guaranteed a hefty loss.
We'll never get our money back no matter how we tried,
Unless you got some brainstorm..." K.T. pondered then replied,
"I reckon we could bill'em... or, if mark ups ain't a crime,
Just charge'em twice the goin' rate at reimplanting time."

VISITING DOGS

When I hear a truck pull up in front of the house and the pandemonium of dogs barkin' would wake a hibernating mastodon, I relax. It's only my neighbor, D. K., come to borrow something of his back.

He doesn't get this ferocious reception because he's on the canine list of unsavory visitors or because he has the reputation of annoying domestic animals on a regular basis. It's because his two dogs usually accompany him on his rounds.

My dogs even bark at his pickup when he drives in anticipating that his dogs will be in the back. On those rare occasions when he comes "undogged", my dogs give him a withering glare and stomp off. It's like they are disappointed.

After all, what else have they got to do? Watch the sheep through the fence? Go to the pasture and check the cows. Sneak up on the creek in hopes of scaring the urea out of the ducks.

I watched them the last time I went to D. K.'s to borrow his brush hog. My dogs were leaning out the side already clearing their throats as we neared his place. I deliberately drove by the first turn-in. Both dogs jerked their heads around and glared at me through the back window. I could see Hattie mouthing the words, "Hey turkey, ya missed it!"

I turned in the second drive and we were met with the raucous sounds of a rabbit let go in a dog kennel. I pulled to a stop as D. K.'s dogs surrounded the pickup barking at the top of their dog lungs.

My dogs were leaning out over the side like seasick fishermen returning in kind, bark for bark. It was deafening.

But I noticed D. K.'s dogs never got quite close enough to touch noses and mine knew just how far to lean to avoid actual contact.

One might think it was all for show. Protecting their territory, as if his were shouting, "Don't you dare get out", and mine were screaming, "No way we're lettin' you jump in this truck!"

Or they could just be visiting like old folks at a reunion, "HOW ARE YOU, TEX! I HEAR YOU GOT A NEW HEARING AID! WHAT KIND IS IT?"

"QUARTER TO FOUR!"

I've gotten to where I don't worry about it much. Dogs like to bark. It's in their job description. It probably doesn't irritate the dogs near as much as it does us humans. They just communicate at different decibel levels. It's part of nature. It's possible even aphids bark at each other and we just can't hear it. But it must drive the ants crazy.

THE PROUD CUT HOLSTEIN STEER

I'll never know just how I got that proud cut Holstein steer.
    I'd rather have lasagna fingers wiggled in my ear
Or get caught eating tofu at the Cattlemen's Hotel
    Than spend another minute with that Holstein steer from Hell.

I put him out to grass with some I'd taken on the gain.
    He soon became the Holstein image of Saddam Hussein.
Most cattlemen I know would never make the same mistake
    'Cause steers like him are meaner than a constipated snake.

One afternoon I drove out to inspect this herd of mine.
    The dog jumped out and vanished, but like stink bait on the line
He soon bobbed to the surface like he'd hooked FREE WILLY's tail,
    Behind him, jaws a 'snappin', came the Holstein killer whale!

I ducked behind a sagebrush but the dog jumped in the cab.
    What followed was a battle like this truck had never had.
Imagine if a coal train pullin' sixty cars in back,
    Doin' ninety miles an hour hit a beer can on the track.

I heard the metal crumple, heard the plastic rip and tear,
    I heard the tires exploding, felt things flyin' through the air.
The dog just kept on barkin' so the steer stayed on the fight,
    Then Lancelot came chargin' up to save me from my plight.

This knight in shining armor was, in fact, to put it blunt,
    My wife in her new tractor with a bale spear on the front.
Distracted by the tractor, the steer came to a stop.
    I raced back to the pickup and clamored up on top.

"Up here!" I hollered loudly, "You can lift me with the spear!"
    The steer came back like bad news, but my wife had heard me clear.
But her aim...(I hollered, "Higher!") was a foot or two off tilt.
    She punched right through the truck door and she rammed it to the hilt!

She pulled back on the lever and we all rose overhead.
    I say 'we all' because the steer had jumped up in the bed.
The last thing I remember just before I pulled the pin
    was Holstein halitosis and the roof a'cavin' in.

I'm still not sure what happened. I was knocked out cold as toast.
    I woke up feelin' dizzy, propped against a cedar post.
The dog was lookin' nauseous there behind the steering wheel,
    The pickup...think Titanic, was a mass of twisted steel.

And what about that proud cut, man eatin', truck stompin', dog kickin',
    Never backin' up polled heavyweight Holstein steer from Hell?
    Well, only time will tell.

But with huntin' season comin' up, his fate is cut and dried.
    He's goin' out to pasture with a bulls-eye on his side.

BOB BLACK '98

BOTH SIDES

Yeah, he wished he was a cowboy
but just at times like this

When he's spent the day a'horseback
and had time to reminisce

Never thinkin' about Monday,
'bout the real life he led

Just the smell of sweaty horses
and the peace inside his head

How he really could'a been one
if the cards had fell that way

But he never had the option
he had other cards to play

And he sees the hired on wranglers
when he passes them the reins

And he almost wants to join 'em
but his common sense refrains

So he joins his boon companions
and they toast their saddle sores

They revel in the cowboy life
and forget the wrangler's chores

But by Monday they're a memory
as he bills another page

And forgets the car he's drivin'
would've paid their yearly wage

Yup, he's glad that he's a cowboy
but there's times on days like this

When he spends all day a'horseback
thinkin', 'wonder what I've missed.'

Never knowin' if it's Monday,
if he'll ever get ahead

Just the smell of sweaty horses
and a blanket for a bed

How he grew up punchin' cattle,
had no other cards to play

So he never had the option,
it was bound to be this way

And he sees the weekend cowboys when
they're handin' him the reins

And he wonders, could he make
it in their life of ball and chains

But he joins his fellow cowboys
and they do their nightly chores

Then doze off while the campfire talk
drifts in from distant shores

But by Monday he's back ridin'
and the open smell of sage

Reminds him he would not survive
in a weekend cowboy's cage

HELPLESS

"I do solemnly swear, as shepherd of the flock, to accept the responsibility for the animals put in my care. To tend to their basic needs of food and shelter. To minister to their ailments. To put their well being before my own, if need be. And to relieve their pain and suffering up to, and including the final bullet.

"I swear to treat them with respect. To always remember that we have made them dependent on us and therefore have put their lives in our hands.

"As God is my witness."

Helpless.

The worst winter in Dakota's memory, 1997. Cattle losses estimated at 300,000 head. And how did they die? From exposure and lack of feed. Basic needs - food and shelter.

Do you think those Dakota ranchers said, "Well, I'll just close down the store and put on the answering machine. We'll wait 'til the storm blows over. No harm done."

No. They couldn't . . . wouldn't.

"Charles, you can't go out there. The cows are clear over in the west pasture. You can't even see the barn from here."

But he tried anyway. Tried to get the machinery runnin', tried to clear a path, tried to load the hay, tried to find the road.

These are not people who live a pampered life. These are not people who are easily defeated. These are not people who quit trying.

But days and weeks on end of blizzards, blowing snow and fatal wind chills took their toll. Cattle stranded on the open plains with no cover, no protection, no feed, no place to go and no relief from the arctic fury, died in singles and bunches and hundreds and thousands, frozen as hard as iron.

Back in the house sat the rancher and his family, stranded. Unable to do what every fiber in his body willed him to do. Knowing that every hour that he could not tend to his cows, diminished him in some deep, permanent, undefinable way. Changing him forever.

The losses were eventually tallied in number of head and extrapolated to dollars. But dollars were not what kept him pacing the floor at night, looking out the window every two minutes, walking out in it fifty times a day, trying, trying, trying.

Exhaustion, blood shot eyes, caffeine jitters, depression, despair....knowing if he only could get to them, he could save them.

Then finally having to face the loss. His failure as a shepherd. That's what kept him trying.

It is hard to comfort a person who has had his spirit battered like that. *"It couldn't be helped." "There was nothing you could do,"* is small consolation. So, all I could say to our fellow stockmen in the Dakotas is,

"In our own way, we understand."

WATER

The big boy land developers hired them a worn out hack
  To go and buy the water rights off farmers down the track.
"Just pay 'em anything they ask. Hell, any price on earth.
  Those farmer's haven't got a clue of what it's really worth."

"Them's fightin' words," the farmer said. *"This water ain't for sale*
  It's all that keeps this place alive. Without it crops would fail."
The lawyer sorta laughed it off. "We'll get it anyway.
  The cities need it all to grow. You can't stand in their way.

It's progress, you should know by now you can't hold back the flood."
  "There's lifetimes given to this land. The water's in their blood."
"Old man that's ancient history, besides we'll make you rich.
  Just name yer price, you'll have it. It's nothin' but a ditch."

"Yer hollow as your vacant eyes. Yer empty as yer word.
  You can't see past the dollar signs. These things that you've inferred
Are bigger than yer lawyer's fee, yer Judas ten percent.
  You've no respect for anything, you covet just the rent.

Go back to your rich puppeteers who've never broke a sweat,
  Who ride in when the battle's done and use their bayonet
To finish off the wounded brave and pick their pockets clean
  Then sell their spoils to innocents to keep their cities green.

Explain to them the difference between value and price.
  That value isn't what is paid it's what is sacrificed
That gives it worth. It's measured in the turns around a field,
  In families and community, in broken bonds and healed,

In barns burnt down and harvest lost and kids gone off to war.
  Explain to them it's measured in grooves worn in your soul... or,
In depths of neighbors breaking hearts when someone's lost a wife,
  And that you can't just set a price on someone's way of life.

NIGHT MAN IN THE HEIFER LOT

I came on just after supper. Boss had fixed a little sheep camp
    with a bed and propane burner so a feller could have coffee
in the middle of the night.

On my first check it was quiet in my bunch of calvy heifers
    and the moonlight made the cedars look like postcards, I was thinkin'
all was good and all was right.

But at ten I found two mamas with their water bags a showin'.
    They were off there in a corner so I left'em to their business
and went back to fill my mug.

In an hour one showed progress. Heifers take a little longer,
    but the other needed checkin' so I worked her to the calvin'
barn and put her in a jug.

Pullin' calves is always chancy like yer playin' slots in Vegas,
    Put yer hand in - pull the lever - double front feet or the head back,
nothin' comin' but the tail.

But tonight my luck was runnin', head and feet were pointin' at me
    so I chained'em up and gently help him make a change of address.
Like deliverin' the mail.

I administered a rub down, swung him upside down a second,
    stuck a straw up to his nostril, watched him fill his lungs unaided
with his first taste of fresh air.

Then I loosed the heifer's halter. She was quick to start his lessons.
    Soon her baby found the fountain, tail a'ringin', he was suckin'
in his calfskin underwear.

By coincidence I noticed back behind in yonder corner
    that the other heifer also had her baby up and suckin'
and was puttin' on a show.

It was sorta satisfyin'. I admit I paused a minute
    to appreciate life's mysteries, although mostly I was thinkin'
only ninety-six to go.

TED'S BIG STEER

Ted and his dad needed some cows to stock their little ranch in Oklahoma, and they needed 'em right away. A local trader solved their problem and injected a couple loads into them.

By fall Ted began to notice one calf that stood taller than the rest. Must'uve had some Chianina blood coursing through his veins. They called him Alf.

They got the big calf castrated and branded and watched him grow like a weed. After several months Ted gathered a bunch to ship. But Alf ducked back. Ted shook out a loop and gave chase.

"Let 'im go!" said Dad, "We'll get him next time!"

Early spring they went to feedin' cake to the herd. Alf was now a yearlin'. Ted kept thinkin' he'd get a rope on him but Alf was too smart.

He'd hang back 'til the truck pulled forward then he'd hit the cake.

"Yer better off just lettin' him go," said Dad. "We'll get him eventually."

Over the next two years Ted became a master of the bait - trap - ambush - sneak attack methods of capturing a wild beast. He actually tricked Alf into a set of corrals only to see him clear the 4 1/2 foot board fence like a hunter-jumper.

His last fall, Alf was big as an army ambulance.

He let himself get gathered with the cows knowing he could escape at will but Bwana Ted had reinforced his alleys making them too high for Alf to jump out of. Ted sorted off all the cows but one leaving her in the alley with Alf.

You could almost hear the chalk squawkin' on the blackboard inside Ted's brain. He backed a closed top stock trailer into one end of the alley and opened the tailgate. He figgered he would take both to the sale if both accidentally loaded. Sure nuf, one loaded. The cow of course!

Alf was circlin' like a hammerhead shark in the shallow end of the pool.

Rust and metal filings flew out Ted's ears as he plotted his next move. With Dad's help as a diversion (bait, some would say), Ted snuck into the back end of the alley driving the tractor with the loader bucket six feet in the air. Suspended from the bucket with chains was an eight foot steel panel. It just cleared the sides of the alley.

Ted drove slowly down the alley until Alf was six feet from the open trailer tail gate. Alf was bouncing off the boards and metal. Splinters flew, welds broke, bolts came loose, cannons boomed, flags fluttered, palm trees bent and waves crashed as Alf turned the earth into a whale wallow!

Ted invoked the cowboy spirit and leaped up into the loader bucket. His eyes blazed with fury, his body tensed, his mind temporarily left the scene of the impending wreck. He was almost eyeball to eyeball with the raging behemoth.

Alf paused in surprise. Ted rose to his full height and screamed at the top of his lungs!

Alf tucked his tail and loaded like a milk pen calf.

When he crossed the scale at the sale the next day, he weighed 1750. Brought nearly a thousand dollars. Dad's still tryin' to talk Ted into gettin' some more like him.

FEEDLOT HEROES

Now and then I get to thinkin' I should quit this feedlot job.
    Go and ride with Buster, what's-his-name, his Texas wagon mob.
Maybe move to old Montana, wear them bat wings for a while
    Or do California daywork in the old vaquero style.

    I get my western magazines, shoot, I keep'em by my chair
        And I read'em after lunchin', sometimes wishin' I was there.
    See, it all looks so romantic. All they do is brand and ride
        Maybe gather up some wild ones, push'em down the other side

While the cameras keep on snappin', set against a scenic view
    Lookin' picturesque and western, quintessential buckaroo.
It's not often that reporters come by here and spend a day
    And the stories that they usually write are mostly exposé

    And I really can't remember any artist incidents.
        All the painters that I've ever seen were workin' on the fence.
    'Cause nobody wants to see us cowboys dressed in overshoes
        In our insulated covies on a feedlot winter cruise,

Sortin' fats in some bleak alley with the mud up to our knees,
    Shovelin' bunks or treatin' sick ones, fightin' flies or allergies.
I take a little nap sometimes, in my chair there after lunch
    And I dream that I am workin' for some rope and ride'em bunch

    Where a roaming photo graffer lookin' for the real thing
        Is dazzled by my cowboyness, the essence of my being.
    And he poses me majestic by the River Babylon
        Mounted on my paint caballo, conchos glistening in the sun.

But at five till one I waken with the image in my mind
    Of the picture he has taken for the cover, but I find
I'm portrayed in all my glory standin' in the chronic pen
    Lookin' at a scruffy lump jaw that needs lancin' once again.

    I get up and grab my jacket that's the color of manure
        And I head back to the feedlot, catch some horses for the shoer,
    But I worry if my heroes in that cowboy magazine
        Ever get a lick of work done, 'cause they always look so clean.

THE VEGETABLE DEFAMATION TRIAL

It was a severe case of vegetable defamation
the makin's of a landmark case of harassment and abuse.
The plaintiff, a Miss Parsley was demanding compensation
of one Paul Pierre Potato and, to-be-specified produce.

"So how do you plead, Mr. Tater?"   "Not guilty but let me relate
I'm a victim of mass inflammation, au gratined and smeared on a plate,
laid next to a lecherous cutlet whose gravy kept touching my cheese.
It was all I could do to keep silent. Then I felt the promiscuous peas.

Nudging their firm little bodies, assuming themselves in my space,
It was clear they had eyes for the cutlet and longed for his gravy embrace.
And there I lay lumpy and fighting my pain, ignored as the fork stirred their lust.
The shame that I felt in their amorous twine sorely tempted, but cry out I must,

'Decorum', I prompted, 'Remember you're food! Presentation is half of the meal!
Take pride in your placement and dress up your ranks, we're the chef's culinary ideal.
A painting in fiber, a sculpture in glaze, a feast for a gourmet's eye view!
You're acting like leftovers, reheated lumps. The diners will think that we're stew.'

Alas, twas no use, they continued to mix 'til we looked like a discarded cud.
Bereft of all pride, depraved by the scene, I peered up out of the mud.
And there on the edge, immune to the drama in which I was hopelessly scrounged,
A vision of verdant vegetaciousness . . . Miss Parsley, provocative, lounged."

"At last," said the judge, "you have got to the point." "Your honor, I meant no offense.
My ardor, my shame, my hope gave me voice and I lost all track of good sense.
I lay in the wallow of half eaten peas, a gristle and gravy abyss,
So I asked, 'Why's a cute little sprig like yourself ensconced on a platter like this?' "

"Is that all?" asked the judge, "That was intentional," Potato replied in retort,
"The plate was slick, I started congealing, I grabbed at her frond for support.
I got cheese on her ramus. She drew back aghast, 'Don't think I've not heard of your couch!
You dirty old tuber, when I'm through with you, you'll wish you were powdered, I'll vouch.'

It only got worse. Said I looked like a chip. Some fast food turned up by a plow.
'A chip!' I decried. 'A step below fried!' She said, 'I'm referring to cow!'
It was all I could take, 'You incipient fern, you nourishment of last resort!
It's no wonder nobody eats parsley.' She said, 'Greaseball, I'll see you in court.' "

Vegetable harassment was the charge the judge adjudicated on.
The retribution swift and a sentence some might think unduly rash
for Potato was convicted and was corned beef hash by dawn
and Miss Parsley was, as usual, just scraped into the trash.

RHINO LOVE

Dr. Fosse, once of Pretoria, commented that most of my stories involved wrecks. I said I think it's the nature of business. "Matter of fact," I said, "You could haul a bunch of cowboys from the U.S. to South Africa, turn'em loose on the savannah and they'd be in a wreck as quick as one of 'em broke out his lasso."

"Actually," he said, "We're quite capable of creating our own." Then he told me about Martha and Arthur, two star-crossed rare white rhinos.

In a governmental gesture of goodwill, South Africa agreed to ship Arthur to Tanzania to mate with Martha. Brilliant veterinarians, competent game management officials, long-winded reproductive specialists and the press discussed at length the procedures involved and the benefits that would accrue with these international relations.

They soon discovered that rhinos cycle according to the length of daylight hours. Martha, on Equatorial Daylight Time, was never quite synchronized with Arthur, on Tropic of Capricornical Time. When he was randy she had a headache and when she was cuddly he was not in the mood.

However, our team of deep thinkers figgered a way around it. They'd artificially inseminate Martha! I can just see these characters squatting under an Acacia tree, breakin' out a case of Congo Lite and drawing their plans in the dirt with pipettes.

But since Martha wasn't cooperating anyway and no sweet smelling rhino geldings were around, they decided to collect Arthur's semen with an electro ejaculator.

Enlisting the aid of their agricultural engineers, they built a homemade ejaculator out of wire, copper electrodes, a hand crank and lots of electrical tape.

Arthur was quite tame so on the big day they led him out with a loop around the horn and tied him to a thorn tree. With proper lubrication, the head mogul inserted the prod and set the cowboys to crankin'. Alas, Arthur showed no response.

"He's probably packed with dry feces which is interfering with conduction of the current," interjected the rhino physiologist.

So they attempted to clean him out while he stood there compliantly. Then they tried again...no luck.

"Being a desert beast, possibly there is a lack of internal moisture," observed the rhino hydrologist. "How 'bout an enema?"

They hung a twenty gallon container from the tree, inserted a hose and the water disappeared like a Diet Sprite in the Sahara. "More water!" they cried. Another twenty gallons were fetched and inserted. Arthur stood unruffled.

Agreeing that should have certainly lubricated Arthur, the chief acting assistant veterinary cowboy technician strode forth and inserted his plastic sleeved arm to evacuate the bowel. Arthur had had enough.

He clamped his powerful aft torpedo door shut just above the hapless white smocked invader's elbow. They thundered off through the brush! The crew followed in the Land Rover, eating their sack lunches and videoing the chase.

A hundred yards down the track the offending appendage popped out followed by 40 gallons of pent up colored water. The invader lay like a drowned muskrat left in the furrow. Arthur raced off to the other side of the game park.

"Yer right," I told Dr. Fosse, "we couldn't have done it better."

MR. DEWEY'S HOOK & CHAIN

I went out with Mr. Dewey, maybe learn a thing or two.
    We motored through the pasture to his cows
Till our path befell a crossing, a trail laid to waste,
    Like forty rhinos passed by pullin' plows.

All the sagebrush had been flattened, great big gouges in the earth,
    Bits of cloth and hair were blowin' in the breeze.
Mr. Dewey hacked a lunger and then felt of his black eye
    Which now looked more the hue of moldy cheese.

"You?" I asked. He nodded, "I was out here yesterday,
    I had to pull a calf, came straight from town.
But I used my regular method, what I call the Hook & Chain,
    Where I sneak up on'em when they're layin' down.

Then I chain their little foot up, slip the hook into a link,
    The big one on the end, you know the one.
Then I put my boot into it, always keep the pressure tight
    That way they never get up till you're done.

"A hook?" I asked, "What kind of hook?" From the rubble on the floor
    He fished a good sized hay hook from the mound.
It was old as grandma's photos and, no doubt it was hand made,
    It looked like some old stirrup that he'd found.

"See, I prop my back against her with my boot there in the hook,
    And push against her when she starts to strain.
I get quite a bit of leverage and they never do get up
    As long as I keep pressure on the chain."

"I see," I said. Though I didn't. I looked back across the trail.
    I could picture what had happened in my mind
When the ol' cow quit the country through the cactus and the rocks
    With Mr. Dewey draggin' 'long behind.

"That explains those nasty bruises and that gash there on yer ear,
    But what went wrong to sabotage yer plot?"
"I was wearin' city footwear, not my mud boots like I should.
    It slipped right through the handle. I got caught.

But you know they never get up, if you keep the pressure on.
    I've proven that a million times before.
And I'll show ya if we spot one that's in need of our assist.
    I've got the chain and hook here on the floor."

Then I glanced down to the floorboard. He was wearin' Birkenstocks!
    "There's one a calvin' now," he said, "just look!"
"So what?" I asked, suspicious, "Well, I see yer wearin' mud boots."
    With that ol' Dewey handed me the hook.

THE SAMARITAN ANGEL

"He's been hurt," cried out the angel, "That ol' counterfeit went down.
I knew that horse was bad news from the start.
Somethin' bad inside is broken. He's just layin' on the ground.
To lose a cowboy always breaks my heart."

"Oh, Father, please forgive me. Can I take back what I said?
It feels like someone's sittin' on my chest.
There's a mutiny inside me that is tearin' off my head.
That pony sure did put me to the test.

Margaret, Margaret! Where's my blanket. Scooch on over here by me.
Who's out there! You ain't foolin' me a bit.
I can hear your chink fringe rattle, step on up where I can see.
That's better. Drag a boulder up and sit.

Yeah, I know my candle's burnin', and I prob'ly should confess,
But I'm mostly missin' Margaret and the crew.
God Almighty are you up there! I have made another mess
And, like always left the cleanin' up for You.

Well, it seems I should do somethin' if that hand on me is Death.
You think a prayer would be appropriate?
'Our Father, who art in Heaven...,' Ah, it's just a waste of breath,
God knows I'm just another hypocrite.

I ain't foolin' anybody. Oop. I feel it comin' now.
Look Mister! There's a bright light over there.
Could you help me off this rock pile, get me on my feet somehow,
It feels like we're just floatin' through the air.

Look! I'm sound as Lee's ol' Traveler. I'm so glad you's passin' by.
You picked pert near the perfect time to come.
How you found me is a wonder. Heaven knows the reason why,
I'm greatful, but just where'd you say yer from?"

"They be comin'," said an angel, "Better saddle up his horse.
He's not the kind to sit around and pine.
His eternity is busy, doin' cowboy work, of course,
And Margaret's comin' someday, he'll be fine."

JOHNNY WAS A MULE MAN

Johnny was a mule man, which says a lot to me.

His motto: keep it simple. Lay it out for me to see.

If a kid can't understand it, it's pro'bly bound to fail.

He'd rather have a good man's word than a contract in the mail.

He never trusted horses or computers on the the shelf,

He'd rather count the cattle, check the pasture for himself.

If he knew you knew your business, he'd back you to the hilt

And gladly give the credit for the fences that you built

But he'd ride you like a blanket so you couldn't go astray

'Cause to him it all was pers'nal . . . he knew no other way.

He didn't have the answers to each problem you were heir

But he figgered you could solve'em. That's why he put you there.

If you could tie a diamond hitch or pour the ol' concrete

That meant as much to him as runnin' out a balance sheet.

See, he knew that all the business in the end came down, somehow

To a single salaried cowboy who went out and checked a cow.

I guess he always thought himself not one of the elite

But a man who works for wages and just got a better seat.

And I'm sure he spent some sleepless nights doubting what he'd done

But he trusted his opinion more than almost anyone's.

So, if he prayed, which most men do, when sleep is closing in,

He pro'bly prayed that Scottish prayer that suited men like him,

"Lord, grant that I am right, that my judgement's not gone blind.

For Thou knowest in Thy wisdom, it's hard to change my mind."

48

HOW DO YOU KNOW IT'S CHRISTMAS?

So, how do you know it's Christmas?

'Cause the sheep can always tell.
    They follow a little tradition and have for quite a spell.
On Christmas Eve around midnight, the sheep, wherever they are
    All rise in quiet unison and fixate on a star.
And from their stirring comes a sound, a chuckling tra, la, la
    That weaves and builds itself into a soft melodious baaa
Which carries like a dove's lament when nights are very still
    As if they're calling for someone beyond a yonder hill.

The legend herders passed on down attributes this tradition
    To one late night in Bethleham. A heavenly petition
Wherein a host of angels came and lured them with a song.
    The herders left in haste, they say, and stayed gone all night long.

Well, sheep don't do too well alone. They've never comprehended
    that on that night they waited up, the world was upended.

So, now when daylight shortens up and nights get long and cold
    I make my check at midnight like we've done since days of old
And if I find the flock intent and standing all around
    I listen for the heavenly host above their throaty sound
And scan the dim horizon in an effort to discern
    The sign the sheep are seeking, that their shepherds will return.

And I am but a watchman in this drama that replays
    Around the earth this time of year, and so I stand and gaze
And though I see no special star or hear no sweet noel,
    I know it must be Christmas, 'cause the sheep can always tell.

SANTY'S EMISSION STICKER

The word came down last Christmas that Santy was not in compliance.
    His mode of transportation fell far short of the standards of science.
The E.P.A. and D.O.T. proclaimed, and here's the real kicker,
    He'd be required to now possess an official emissions sticker.

So off he went to Fort McMurray, the nearest inspection station.
    He drove his team in through the door and was met by a congregation
Of worker ants and clipboard kings all looking so officious.
    "Connect the hoses!" the head man said. The reindeer got suspicious.

"And be aware of pressure leaks, those backfires can be brutal.
    Now rev the RPMs up high and we'll check the whole caboodle."
The carbon dioxide blinking lights began illuminating.
    "A direct result," the inspector said, "of reindeer ruminating.

"The methane levels must be checked out to protect from global warming."
    "Relax," said Santy, "the after burners will keep the methane conforming."
"Just one more test," the inspector said, "to check for particulate matter."
    He kicked the RPMs on up. All thirty-two hooves made a clatter.

"You better back off," Santy shouted... but too late. The tragic result;
    The hoses blew and the reindeer flew like jets off a catapult!
The blast blew out all the windows, eclipsed the A. Borealis.
    Lit up the Kremlin in Moscow and darkened the streets of Dallas.

It knocked the moon outta orbit and started an Arctic tsunami.
    It broke up a mortician party, just when it was gettin' embalmy.
A mushroom cloud arose from the scene, a silent but deadly convector,
    Below, knee deep in emissions stood the intrepid inspector.

He gathered up his dignity with a minimum of swearin'.
    Then with the edge of his clipboard and the hard hat he'd been wearin',
He collected the solid particulates to complete ol' Santy's packet
    By scrapin' the requisite samples off the front of his jacket.

THE THERAPEUTIC GOAT

Goat: 1) The most widely domesticated ruminant in the world
     2) Cantankerous person, as in "Old Goat"
     3) Ancient canon thought to ward off equine disease

Blaine was in Saskatchewan adding to his revolving horse collection, when the seller suggested he take a goat along as well. "Ya know, they have a calming effect on horses. As well as disease prevention."

"Where might I get one?" inquired Blaine. "I have one right here for only $25," replied the seller, injecting ol' Billy into the innocent Blaine. Goat and horse climbed into the trailer.

On the trip home to Pincher Creek Blaine became aware of Billy's strong, some would say unpleasant, odor. It only disappeared when he got above 60 km/h.

Billy became king of the barnyard. He spent time with his original equine companion but generously made himself available to the other horses as well as occasional bulls that required goat therapy.

Blaine was pleased with the harmony that Billy lent to the homestead. And, if the smell bothered Blaine, he never said. It is entirely possible that Blaine was olfactorily impaired due to his constant exposure to the purulent, putrifying parasitic infestations and assorted unsavory, malodorous pestilence that occurred in his daily practice of veterinary medicine.

However, it became a constant source of inquiry by farmers bringing stock by the clinic, as in, "O-o-o-o-e-e-e! Vat's dat smell, eh?"

"It's a goat," explained Blaine, "It's been said they have curative powers." "Yer ta vet," they'd say, "You don't belief dat do you?" You could hear the fear in their voices as they imagined Blaine sending stinking ol' Billy home with them as companion for their trembling llama.

Soon, female goats were added to the menagerie as company for Billy. Goats begat goats begat more goats. The ate everything is sight. When they reached their peak population, the mob numbered 27. They would swarm a full grown conifer or decorative hedge like locusts and strip it bare. Finally under threat of banishment from the house, Blaine got rid of all the goats except Billy, who continued to reign supreme from his throne atop a round bale feeder in the colt corral.

One afternoon a buyer came by to look at some colts. Blaine led him into the corral. Billy was ensconced on his perch, head peaking through the tubular steel frame.

"Whoeee! What in the blasphemous, offensive, scatological, politically incorrect bodily function is that!" the buyer asked, covering his burning eyes and holding his nose. "It's a goat," said Blaine. "It smells dead," choked the buyer.

Blaine gave a second look. Billy was sitting where he always sat, right on top of the round bale feeder. Except his head was at an odd angle where it poked under the steel. Upon closer examination there were other indicators of an accidental barnyard suicide of several days duration, like a balloonish appearance and slippin' of the hair. "Yer right," said Blaine pausing, "I thought that bale was lastin' longer than usual."

R.C. & BUD

R.C. is an animal lover. Maybe not the kind of animal lover that the term has come to mean in this era of animal rights activism, but the kind that requires a greater commitment.

He would tell you he's a farmer. But he's a horseman and trainer, cattleman, hog producer, corn grower and great-grandfather. He's also a dog man, with the patience and persistence to deserve a good stock dog.

R.C. has had a wide variety of dogs in his life. One day he asked his wife, Doris, to keep an eye out for a Blue Heeler. They appealed to him but he'd never had one. 'Kinda rough dogs,' he thought.

Soon she found one advertised in the Albia paper; a two year old male lookin' for a home. R.C. was suspicious. Takin' on a dog that old was risky. Bad habits would be developed, old loyalties established. One just never knew.

"Well, it wouldn't hurt to look," Doris chided him.

Finally, three weeks later R.C. went by to look at the dog. As Doris was introducing themselves to the lady of the house, the two year old blue merle walked right up to R.C. and looked at him. They exchanged studious looks - something unspoken passed between them. R.C. picked the dog up under his arm and took him to the truck.

He just knew. The way some people know when a guitar string is in tune or a steak is cooked just right. R.C. knew the dog would be fine. And, I think the dog must have come to the same conclusion because they became constant outdoor companions. He named him Bud.

Two months after Bud had moved in with them, R.C. was out feeding. He slung a bushel basket of ear corn over his shoulder and walked into the pig pen. Bud was dawdling by the gate.

Sixteen sows came squealing from the corner as R.C. approached. His foot hit something. He slipped, went down on his back, cracked his head on a rock, and was knocked unconscious.

His last memory as he fell was a three ton wall of hungry sows charging.

He woke to find himself looking skyward in the pig pen with sticky blood on his face, in his hair and on his shirt. Bud had worn a circle around his sprawled out body. Just a few feet away the sows waited, watching, a dark look in their eyes. Several ears of corn still lay by his head. Bud stood guard.

Another true dog story like we hear so often. If R.C. had not been an animal lover, would it have had a different ending?

But from their first meeting, dog and man somehow sensed that they would be there for each other. I can't explain how it works, it's beyond me. But it wasn't beyond Bud . . . he just knew.

SALESMAN'S DILEMMA

I had sold a magic bolus to a farmer.
     It was guaranteed to rid his herd of flies
It would pass out with the pucky
     and if everyone got lucky
It would kill the eggs the flies laid in the pies.

     He had bought enough to do a hundred critters.
          "These had better work," he said, "They cost enough."
     "I can guarantee they'll do it,
          I'll come out and take you through it,
     You just follow the directions for the stuff."

I drove out and found the farmer nearly finished
     But the scene I saw sent shivers up my spine
Was the A.I. tech invited?
     Had the farmer grown near sighted?
'Cause a crowd was gathered 'round the cow's behind.

     In the middle wearin' goggles and a slicker
          Smeared with green effluent like he'd hit the fan,
     Dressed in pre-composted splendor,
          Poised at ready to rear-end her,
     Stood the farmer with a balling gun in hand.

"How's it goin', boys," I asked with trepidation.
     "Well, this bothers some cows more than I'd 'uve thought.
This procedure don't impress her."
     I said, "Try a tongue depressor."
But I knew that all his work had been for naught.

     So I watched him put the bolus,...I can't say it.
          My commission check was goin' up in smoke.
     I was gonna take a skinnin'
          Then the whole crew started grinnin'
     And I realized they'd staged it as a joke!

At the office when I told my boss the story
     He got livid, said I'd bolluxed up the sale,
"Now we'll have to go redo'em,
     What the heck did you say to'em?"
"Well, since they only had ten left... I held the tail."

ALL RANCH RODEO

'Twas a matchup made in Elko for the cowboys in the know
Called the Rough and Ready Knock Down Finals All Ranch Rodeo.
Now the Texans entered up a team they thought could never lose
When they bet their reps against the Jordan Valley Buckaroos.

You could tell from where they hailed if you put 'em up for bids,
All the buckaroos wore fancy scarves and Amish lookin' lids
While the Texans wore their jackets for the brush down in the draws
And them twenty dollar roll-yer-own, cheap Guatemalan straws.

It was Blucher versus Leddy, it was leggin's versus chinks
It was rye versus tequila, it was leppies versus dinks,
It was sagebrush versus cactus, it was ear tick versus fly,
It was Poco Bueno versus sloggers raised on alkali.

The Texans took an early lead, at ropin' showed their stuff,
But the buckin' horse fandango showed the buckaroos were tough.
They branded in a dead heat, but in deference to the crowd
Both sides were harshly penalized for cussin' so dang loud.

So the teams were standin' even when the final contest came,
UNTAMED UNGULATE EXTRACTION, wild cow milkin', by name.
They loosed the beasts together, left their calves to bawl and mill
And the two teams fell upon 'em like hyenas on a kill.

The buckaroo a'horseback threw his forty-footer right.
He dallied just about the time the Texan's rope came tight.
Their trajectories collided in a bawlin', buckin' wreck,
The ropes and cows got tangled and they wound up neck to neck.

In the meantime two big muggers plus two milkers brave and bold
Attacked the knot of thrashing hide and tried to get ahold
Of somethin', hoof or horn or foot or spur or can of snoose.
Then, by accident some dummy turned the bawlin' calves a'loose!

There was hair and teeth and eyeballs in the picture now and then,
There was moustache lips and swingin' bags, some thought they saw a hen
Flashin' briefly through the dust cloud. Wild images remain;
A painting done in cow manure, a mating sandhill crane.

To describe the cataclysm would create an overload,
But a photograph was taken and this is what it showed;
At the summit pointed skyward were the Texas mugger's toes,
One arm around a buckaroo, his fingers in his nose,

Who, in turn was mounted sideways splayed acrost a bally black
Who was layin' on a milker who was smashed flat on his back.
The braymer cow was balanced on her head amidst the jag,
While a Texan fought her baby for possession of the bag.

From the cyclone flew two milkers, bottles high for all to see
Like two winos at a party where the wine and cheese was free.
The buckaroo's hind leg was draggin' like he'd lost the farm,
But he kept his place by clingin' to the Texan's broken arm.

When they fell across the finish line and tumbled in the dirt
The judge declared the buckaroo the winner by a squirt.
Since the race looked pert near even, the judge said with a shrug,
"The winner is the cowboy with the most milk in his jug!"

"I object!" cried out the Texan, "Our ol' cow just had three tits!"
"That's a handicap," the judge said, "I admit it's sure the pits,
But in fairness to the buckaroo who dallys for his kicks,
If you added all his fingers, he could barely count to six!"

A few words from the Author ...

Baxter Black

I assume that folks who buy this book are familiar with my previous books and find them useful for wrapping fish or starting fires. As one feller said, "At least it's on smooth paper."

But if you are being exposed to my ultraviolet wit for the first time, you may have realized why artwork is so important in my marketing strategy.

This book, like my others, relies heavily on my good cowboy cartoonist friends, i.e. if you like the drawing, you might read the poem. It's a joint effort of artistry and words. It's about our world - the livestock business. And it's mostly funny 'cause ours is a world where it seems you have to laugh to keep from cryin'.

You get a little glimpse of the cowboy way of doin' things. You might even get stepped on or step in somethin'. It could cause you to wonder why anybody would live like this. We wonder too sometimes. But here we'll stay on the fringe of civilization, hands on the plow, feet in the earth, eyes to the sky, too poor to quit and too proud to listen to the voice of reason.

About the Artists ...

Three-time winner of the prestigious Paisley Snood Award for the least popular novella written during a drought year (most recently - *Nerves of Lard* - Bench Press, 1996) and the lead subject of Hoffman's *Nature's Greatest Genetic Blunders* - Faux Pas Press, 1997 Bob just says, "Hey, we learn from our missteaks."

He lives with his wife, Stephanie, and daughter, Samantha, in central Arizona and sweats for a living.

Bob Black

Don has forsaken all other means of legitimate employment except artwork. A foolhardy decision moderated in part by the cowboy's golden parachute, a wife with a job. Bless Denise.

Since becoming a full time artist he has found himself with more time on his hands. So, he acts as groom, soccer mom and fashion consultant to kids Hailey and Jordan.

Don has also accepted managership of the Gooding, Idaho County Fair, another high paying, part time source of sleepless nights. But his good cowboy attitude prevents any serious side effects from overexertion.

Don Gill

Charlie Marsh

Charlie likes to draw cowboys, horses and cattle, especially in wild action scenes where the cowboy's life is made miserable or perilous by the cross purposes of the critters. He ropes calves and works with cattle, so he knows well these wrecks are not accidents but are part of a premeditated and diabolical plan to rid the cowboy of all virtue and sanity.

He lives in remote southwestern Oklahoma with his wife Laurie, two ravenous dogs, five spoiled cats and a wore out truck.

ARE YOU READY FOR SOME MORE GREAT BAXTER BLACK STORIES AND POETRY?

BOOKS ....

COYOTE COWBOY POETRY 1986
CROUTONS ON A COW PIE, VOL 2 1992
DUNNY AND THE DUCK © 1994
HEY, COWBOY, WANNA GET LUCKY? (CROWN PUB) © 1994
COW ATTACK © 1996
CACTUS TRACKS (CROWN PUB) © 1997

VIDEO TAPES ....

BAXTER'S FIRST VIDEO
BAXTER BLACK BY HIMSELF
BAXTER BLACK LIVE ON PUBLIC TV

AUDIO TAPES ....

THE BAXTER BLACK 4-PAK
    ... INCLUDES ...   BAXTER BLACK LIVE
                              BAXTER BLACK & FRIENDS
                              GENERIC COWBOY POETRY
                              THE BUCKSKIN MARE

THE BAXTER BLACK BOX SET
    ... INCLUDES ...   BAXTER BLACK LIVE UPTOWN
                              BAXTER BLACK LIVE AT THE GRANGE
                              COWBOY PRIDE
                              BAXTER BLACK BUCKS OFF

IF YOU CAN'T FIND ANY OF THESE ITEMS AT YOUR LOCAL BOOKSTORE, CHECK YOUR LOCAL CO-OP, VETERINARIAN, FEED STORE, WESTERN WEAR STORE OR GIVE US A CALL .... (800-654-2550)